better together*

*This book is best read together, grownup and kid.

a kids book about racism™

by Jelani Memory

a
kids
book
about™

Library of Congress Cataloging-in-Publication Data is available.

This book represents my personal experience and thus is not intended to be representative of every form or example of racism as it applies to the many who have experienced it in their lives.

A Kids Book About Racism is exclusively available online on the a kids book about website.

To share your stories, ask questions, or inquire about bulk purchases (schools, libraries, and non-profits), please use the following email address:

hello@akidsbookabout.com

www.akidsbookabout.com

ISBN: 978-1-951253-00-4

Printed in the USA

For my son Solomon

Intro

We "grownups" try to teach kids as much as possible as they grow up. Things like: how to say your ABCs, ride a bike, and when to say "please" and "thank you." And even bigger things, like how to date, when to quit something, and how to forgive. But there are a handful of important topics we often never get around to talking about. Things that are simply too hard to just bring up.

Racism is one of those topics.

And yet, what age is too early for kids to learn about racism? When is "too soon" for kids to learn about how to treat those who look different? Who is supposed to help kids learn about racism?

This is a book designed to help get the conversation started. To help grownups and kids alike wade into a really tough topic and hopefully spark the first of many conversations to come about racism. Enjoy!

This is a book about **racism.**

For reals!

And yes, it really is for kids.

It's a good book to read
with a grownup.

Because you'll have lots to talk about afterward.

(Just you? Keep reading. The book won't **BITE!**)

Now to introduce myself...

My name is **Jelani.**

My skin color looks like

this.

(If you're colorblind, "**this**" is the color brown.)

Because my Dad is

black.

And my Mom is

white.

Which makes me...

mixed.

Or...

**African American,
biracial,
black,
or a person of color.**

I'm proud of who I am and the color of my skin.

But,

because of my skin color,
people aren't always nice to me.

Sometimes I get called names.

Other times it's **worse.**

The person doing it
might not even realize
that it **hurts** me...

A LOT!

And when they treat me that way,
it makes me feel...

small.

You see,
some people believe
that having different color skin
means you aren't as good as others.

That's called...

racism.

What is racism?

Racism means
to hate someone,
exclude them,
or treat them badly
because of their race,
or the color of their skin.

racism racism racism racism racism
racism racism racism racism racism racism
racism racism racism racism racism racism
racism racism racism racism racism
racism racism racism racism racism
racism racism racism racism racism
racism racism racism racism
racism racism racism
racism racism
sm

And it happens all the time.

rac
racism
rac
ism
rac
racism racism
ism racism
racismracism racism racism
racism racism
racism racism
racism ra
racism racism
smracismracism

racism racism racism racism
racism racism racism racism
racism racism racism racism
cism racism racism racism
sm racism racism racism
cism racism racism racism
racism racism racism
racism racism racism
racism racism racism
cism racism racism
racism racism racism
racism racism racism
racism racism racism
racism racism
m
racism racism
racism racism racism
mracism racism racism
m racism racism racism
m racism racism racism
acismracism racism
racism racism racism
sm racism racism
racism racism
sm racism racism
racism racism
racism racism
racism racism

Not just in **BI**

ways,

but
sometimes
it
shows
up
in
small
ways.

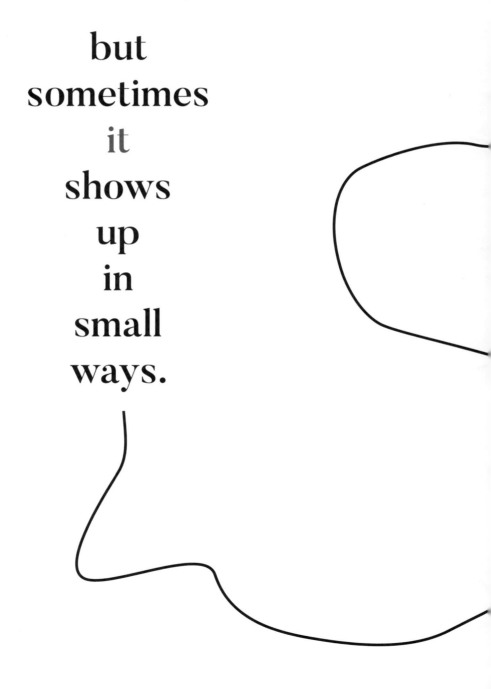

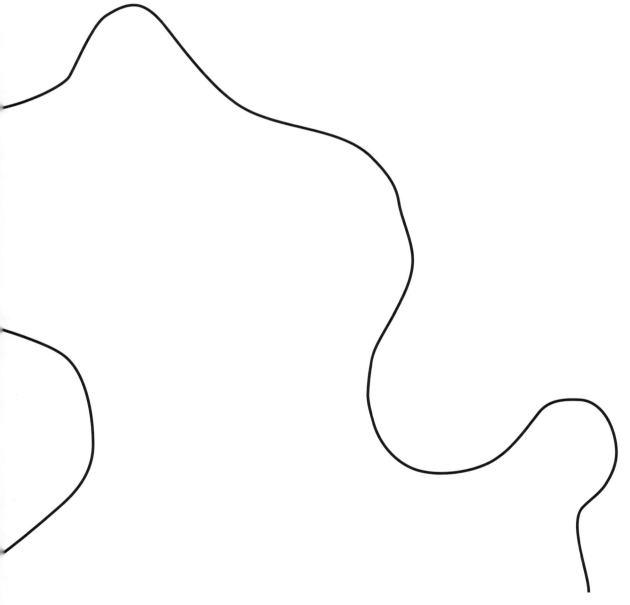

Ways that are almost invisible.

Like...

a look,
a comment,
a question,
a thought,
a joke,
a word,
or a belief.

Racism is one of the worst kinds of mean someone can be.

Because racism thinks being different is bad.

JT,

being **different** is actually good!

Like really, really...

really, really, really, really, really, really, re
really, really, really, really, really, really, rea
really, really, really, really, really, really, re
really, really, really, really, really, really, re
really, really, really, really, really, really, rea
really, really, really, really, really, really, re
really, really, really, really, really, really, re
really, really, really, really, really, really, rea
really, really, really, really, really, really, re
really, really, really, really, really, really, re
really, really, really, really, really, really, rea
really, really, really, really, really, really, r
really, really, really, really, really, really, rea
really, really, really, really, really, really, rea
really, really, really, really, really, really, rea
really, really, really, really, really, really, re
really, really, really, really, really, really, r
really, really, really, really, really, really, re
really, really, really, really, really, really, re

y, really, really, really, really, really, really,
, really, really, really, really, really, really,
ly, really, really, really, really, really, really,
y, really, really, really, really, really, really,
, really, really, really, really, really, really,
ly, really, really, really, really, really, really,
y, really, really, really, really, really, really,
, really, really, really, really, really, really,
ly, really, really, really, really, really, really,
ly, really, really, really, really, really, really,
, really, really, really, really, really, really,
lly, really, really, really, really, really, really,
y, really, really, really, really, really, really,
y, really, (almost there, I promise), really,
, really, really, really, really, really, really,
y, really, really, really, really, really, really,
lly, really, really, really, really, really, really,
ly, really, really, really, really, really, really,
, really, really, really, really, really good!

1000%

od

Because being different means we have so much **MORE** to offer each other.

Things like...

help,

ideas,

strength,

skills,

creativity,

life,

patience,

respect,

community,

love,

knowledge,

experience,

perspective,

insight,

diversity,

wisdom,

empathy,

and originality.

That whole being
different thing,

it makes us better.

Much better!

So if you see someone being
treated badly, made fun of,
excluded from playing,
or looked down on
because of their
skin color...

call it racism.

Outro

Now that you've made it to the end of the book, what comes next? Well, if you're a grownup who read this to a kid, my hope is a lot! They should have a million questions for you, like "Has anyone ever been racist to you?" Or, "Do some people not like me because of the color of my skin?" Take their curiosity and make the most of it.

I can promise you that you're more afraid than they are to talk about racism. So, talk about your experience with racism, or that of your friends. Talk about our country's history and the civil rights movement. And above all, be honest. Kids are ready and willing to learn about tough things, if only the grownups present in their lives are willing to talk about them.

find
more
kids
books
about

belonging, feminism, creativity
money, depression, failure,
gratitude, adventure,
cancer, body image,
and mindfulness.

 **akidsbookabout.com**

share your read*

*Tell somebody, post a photo, or give this book away to share what you care about.

@akidsbookabout